TURN YOUR PASSION INTO PROFIT

DISCOVER THE 5 SECRET FORMULAS TO SUCCESS

"You're not born to just pay bills and die!"

*Discover the 5 Secret Formulas
of how I transformed $5 into a 6-figure income,
working from home – even after my doctors said,
I will not be able to walk anymore.*

Celebrity Author, Global Speaker, Life Coach
CEO & Founder, www.StepUpJourney.com

ZAI MIZTIQ

ISBN
Paperback 979-8-89588-967-1
Hardcase 979-8-89984-557-4

This book has been published with all efforts taken to make the material error-free after the consent of the author. However, the author and the publisher do not assume and hereby disclaim any liability to any party for any loss, damage, or disruption caused by errors or omissions, whether such errors or omissions result from negligence, accident, or any other cause.

While every effort has been made to avoid any mistake or omission, this publication is being sold on the condition and understanding that neither the author nor the publishers or printers would be liable in any manner to any person by reason of any mistake or omission in this publication or for any action taken or omitted to be taken or advice rendered or accepted on the basis of this work. For any defect in printing or binding the publishers will be liable only to replace the defective copy by another copy of this work then available.

Dedication

In the name of the Most Merciful and Most Compassionate - Allah. I dedicate this book to a special person in my life, my role model, pillar of strength, and my best friend.

She may not have received any education from a school, but she is able to converse in five different languages. When she speaks, it is like water overflowing without barriers.

She never had a job, yet we are blessed to have been spared from hunger and homelessness. She single-handedly raised six children without whining or complaining at any moment of her life. She is a woman of wisdom, a warrior princess, and an overflowing fountain of love, and I reciprocate that love back to her - **she is my Mother**.

Contents

Writer's Note

As mentioned in the book of Michael Heart, *The Most Influential People*, Prophet Muhammad (peace and blessings be upon him and his family) was credited to be the most influential man in history. In this book, I will quote the Prophetic Tradition and narration of Prophet Muhammad (peace and blessings be upon him and his family) — He is our ultimate role model sent to us as a Mercy for The Universe. Each quote in this book will guide us through discovering the five secret Formula of Success with the elements of **T.R.U.T.H.** It is going to be exciting and enjoyable as you beat the odds and do what your heart tells you to do. Just don't forget to have fun along the way.

Yours truly,

A few years ago, I broke my spine, but it did not break my spirit. I realised that life had to go on. I decided to turn my pain into power and set out on a mission to empower, educate and enrich humanity.

If you are a person who wants to be happy in this lifetime, step out of your comfort zone and seek beneficial knowledge to upgrade your skills and increase your zest for life.

One key ingredient to a happy and fulfilled life: **"Think with your heart, strategise in your mind, and take massive action with your limbs."**

What Our Readers Say

"Dear Zai, Once again, congratulations on the publication of your book. Listening to you, I feel greatly inspired too. I am sure that young people will be inspired by your story."

Mdm. Halimah Yacob

President of the Republic of Singapore

"Dear Zai, I'm loving your books! It feels like you've beautifully captured your thoughts and feelings in a way that deeply resonates with me. Reading them makes me feel like I know you personally. I believe these books can inspire and connect with so many others who are looking for guidance and empowerment."

Ms. Prabh Kaur (India)

"To say Miss Zai is amazing would be an understatement – she's a powerhouse. As a young woman of 25, I am in awe of everything she has accomplished over the years. Our connection ignited a fire in me to strive to be a better woman in my own journey. It's clear that the only limits we face as women are the ones we place on ourselves."

Fridah Mwakoi (Kenya)

"Miss Zai has a natural stage presence and speaks not just to the mind but to the heart. Her words are simple yet deeply intentional, making her message accessible and impactful. There's no unnecessary jargon—just authentic communication. She speaks from lived experience, not theory. Her wisdom, softened by her sense of humour, made her relatable to everyone, no matter their background."

Professor Kgoaile (South Africa)

"Reading this book was absolutely awesome and life-changing. The insights and guidance provided helped me see things from a new perspective, and I left feeling more empowered and focused on my goals. Zai's approach was not only informative but also deeply inspiring, making me feel supported and ready to take on new challenges. Highly recommend for anyone looking to transform their life and mindset! I'm fully ready to do things in my power to change the story of my life & my family. Breakthrough has come over Nigeria. Nigeria is blessed."

Mr. Olafimihan Olatunji (Nigeria)

"Zai gave me a wake-up call and shared her experience to find our purpose, scaffolding the session into actionable steps. I love to listen to her speak from her heart, so genuine and with 22 years plus experience in entrepreneurship, that is a bonus! Imagine someone's compiling their ups and *down, shortcut to happiness and success, and share the tips with you. That is Zai for you."*

Miss Nabihah Hashim *(Malaysia)*

"Miss Zai's work is nothing short of transformational. Her insights on turning past pain into strength, knowing your purpose, and building influence with intention were deeply impactful. Zai's passion, wisdom, and energy brought incredible fire to the room. Highly recommend her to anyone seeking clarity, confidence, and direction in their personal or professional journeys."

Ikionana Ezekiel *(Nigeria)*

"Reading it opens one's mind. Understanding the message, opens one's heart. Few people we know have the courage to pick up from pieces and become whole again. So, when a story of such fate comes along, it is a must-read. I find the strength in Zai as an exemplary model.

"Courage is not sexist, and her journey is not just geography. The sharing in the book now inadvertently makes Zai an icon for a comeback story, a fact-over-fiction story, and a story that everyone needs a little reminding of in challenging times.

"I congratulate Zai for being the soul-guardian for many of us who are still searching. Before reaching the last page, you will probably find that what you are looking for has been with you all along. I do."

Mr. Fahmi Rais

Former CEO of Suria TV Channel, Singapore

"Dear sis, you are doing a great job! After reading your book, the after-effect feeling I had was like nothing in life is difficult or impossible to do. It is us and us only. It is our perception of the things around us and it leads to what we are now.

"Your life experiences, love for your mum, love for nature, and the confidence you have in yourself aptly relates and connects the message you are trying to tell your readers. It is a wake-up call and it makes me think about what I have achieved so far and why I have been thinking in a certain way all this while. There are more feelings other than this which I can't describe in words. The feeling is beautiful.

"In summary, after reading your book, it gives me confidence to be a multi-millionaire in this world and a billionaire in the Hereafter. It is ACHIEVABLE."

Nafisah Kassim (Singapore)

"I just completed reading your book. I have no words to describe the after feeling and the effect it gives me. It is simply marvellous. The message put across very aptly with life examples! I am so proud of you, sis! Looking forward to more such books from you and may your success reach greater heights. Ameen."

Hayati Eusofe

"Awesome book with amazing formula to success. Once you start reading, you cannot stop. I'm loving every single word written. So powerful that I got mesmerized by it."

Siti Humairah

"Zai is not an ordinary person; this alone is very interesting. From her book, you will see why she is so exceptional and why there is so much we can learn from her life experience, her attitude, her insights. And much more. Referring to your book now and then really helps."

Mr. Casey Ong (Singapore)

Former Director of Service Source Inc

Introduction

Do you realise that every single person has the freedom to experience both joy and challenges in life? What would life be without its drama? Without its dreams? Yet, what use are dreams if we intentionally refuse to turn them into reality? Living life to the fullest has always been my mantra. I thrive on spontaneity, on creating something entirely new, and embracing the gladness, sadness, and madness that comes with being human.

The key to truly living is learning to think beyond the ordinary. One defining moment for me came when I was 20, fresh out of college. Unlike my peers who pursued degrees, I chose a different path. I left Singapore and set out to become a busking henna artist in Japan. It was a bold decision, but life had other plans. The bitter cold of winter made street art nearly impossible. I found myself at a crossroads: should I catch the next flight home to enjoy the warmth of the sun, or stay and push through despite the harsh conditions?

In that moment, I chose to follow my heart, despite the obstacles. This book is about those moments—when we choose to step into the unknown and embrace the journey. It's for the aspiring entrepreneurs, young or old, who need a spark of contagious energy, who are searching for a fresh perspective. If you're ready to make a difference and follow the path of transformation, this book is for you.

I live by a few guiding principles. I always see the glass as half full. Like a river, I flow with life. Ideas, to me, are like the strokes of an artist's brush on a blank canvas. Whether you're staring at an empty page or moulding a piece of clay, the possibilities are endless. The sky is the limit—if you believe in the boundless power of God, you'll understand that His abundance is limitless.

We must embrace the freedom we've been given to explore life's endless possibilities without holding ourselves back. The only true limit is the one we place on ourselves—self-doubt and fear of the unknown. But with persistence, fine-tuning, and a willingness to grow, we can break free from those restraints. Remember, everyone has the freedom to laugh, cry, and express their emotions. It's part of what makes us human.

This is the Way of Life

We are all living within the circle of life, connected by threads of continuity. Each of us has been created for a purpose. We are brought to this Earth to be part of something far greater than ourselves – a family, a team, an organisation, a global community, the very Cosmos itself.

By now, you should feel deeply aware of the limitless and timeless nature of human connectivity. The time has come for you to respond with urgency to what is in front of you. It's now or never! The only question you need to ask is, "Where do I begin? And how do I get there?"

Since my journey began in 2001, I've navigated the highs and lows, the hard knocks and the heartwarming moments. Along the way, I've gained valuable insights and strategies for building a successful, purpose-driven business. But the greatest challenge I've seen time and again is this: the courage to rise up and ignite your passion and your God-given talents. For some of you, that fire is already burning; for others, it's a treasure waiting to be uncovered.

I am here to help you do just that. I will guide you to unlock your potential and share with you the five Secret Formulas to Turn Your Passion into Profit. This truth-based formula will lead you on a path of self-discovery, self-appreciation, and potentially, the journey to becoming the next self-made millionaire.

Who is Zai Miztiq?

Zai Miztiq was born and raised in Singapore. Since she was young, she had this creative skill that made money for her. She rarely asked her parents for a school allowance. She loves art. She would buy coloured papers and pens from her savings and would make bookmarks to sell them to her schoolmates at recess and in between breaks. She would go from one class to another, make friends with the head monitor to promote her 'arts and crafts' ideas. Every month she would churn out a new product line to stay fresh in the 'market'. The most unforgettable thing that she made and sold was 'paper slippers'. They were not wearable, but people loved the designs and paid for them. At that tender age, when most of her friends would run out of school towards the ice-cream stand, attempting to finish their daily pocket money, Zai was walking home with a heavy pocket full of coins and a light heart full of joy.

Zai has always believed that money does not make money. Ideas make money. All of her businesses started with little or no money.

With her passion for henna art, in 2001, Zai set up 'Miztiq Henna & Body Art' aiming to teach the art of henna and provide henna decoration services for any occasion. The venture was not just a money-making deal; it was an interest that Zai fervently calls her 'first love'.

After three years of hard work, her endeavour was at its peak. She was invited to teach henna art in Japan and was featured in Japanese magazines throughout the country. Living in the 'land of the rising sun' for half a year, Zai returned home, welcomed by numerous media interviews. The success story in Japan eventually reached her hometown. Zai then invited her Japanese students to visit Singapore to do a henna art demonstration. As a result, overwhelming publicity boosted her brand. Her business boomed so fast that Zai started receiving bookings for bridal henna art two years in advance. Customers were delighted and satisfied with her excellent work and service. Concurrent with running her booming business, she sought out other opportunities to invest in. It was at the peak of her success that a calamity occurred, challenging her character, motivation, and even her will to live on.

It happened on a warm and sunny afternoon of April 22, 2005, at about 4:44 in the afternoon when Zai was heading home. Riding in a taxi, hungry and exhausted, wishing that life could be easier on her, forgetting that she had a happy family, great friends and a successful business. Eight minutes from home, thinking about the warm meal her mum had prepared for her, her life came to a standstill. A bang so loud that it felt like time had stopped, her taxi slammed into the back of a huge army trailer. She tried reaching for the taxi door but she could barely move. In extreme pain, she tried reaching for her cell phone but the effort was to no avail. At that instance, she thought, "Is this it?" "Is this the end of me?" "Am I going to die today?" - "It cannot be."

For Zai, she felt that she had not done much in life. Her mother still needed her. In short, she was not prepared to die!

Before long, still semi-conscious and helpless, she was taken out of the taxi by three strong men, laid on the stretcher, carried, and placed in an ambulance. By then, she had completely surrendered – no attempt to verify what had just happened or where she was being taken.

Being put through numerous medical observations, X-rays, and CT scans, Zai had to undergo immediate surgery. In excruciating pain, she advised the medical team to proceed with the operation.

Only later did she find out that despite undergoing all the surgical procedures, she had to accept the dreadful fact that she could be paralysed for life. After the surgery, she was prescribed self-controlled morphine for pain management. She would take doses just to turn from right to left to prevent bedsores. Just imagine how painful and uncomfortable it was!

A report by a medical specialist stated: "Zai had experienced a fractured dislocation on her T12/L1. Her other injuries were a right 6th rib fracture and a left foot 5th metatarsal fracture. A posterior instrumentation and fusion from T11 to L3 was done." In other words, she had two metal rods fixed on her spine and eight metal screws 'drilled' into her bones. "The other injuries were managed conservatively. She will be experiencing low back pain for a lifetime. She suffered a very serious injury to the spine. She is fortunate to escape with no gross paralysis. However, she will be left with chronic disabling pain."

By rights, she should be pleased that her life was spared. However, honestly, at that time she had no clue whether to feel joyful or miserable.

For one whole year, Zai dreadfully lived her life with no direction. She had the victim mindset as she recollected those moments. It took her almost a year to recuperate and get back on her feet again. She knew she was meant for greater things, and setbacks like these should not stop her from fulfilling her dreams.

Then Zai wrote a mission statement to herself, a mantra she lives by up to the present: "It is up to you to be a victim or a victor. You may have a physical disability, but you are still gifted with a sound mind and a strong, loving heart to take action. Give thanks for life, help yourself, and move on to help others."

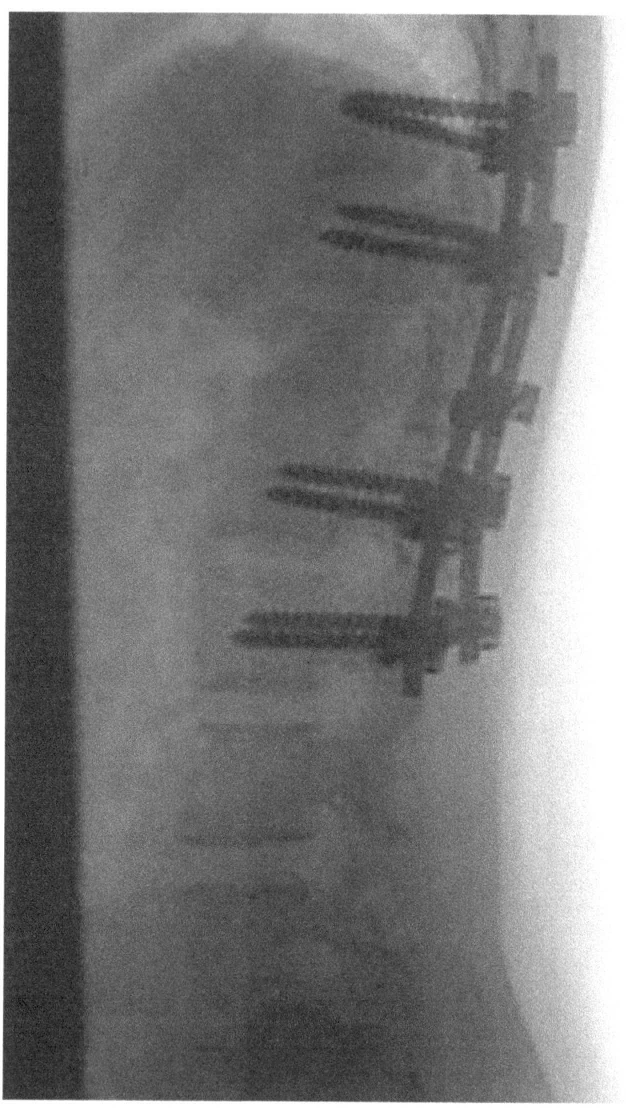

An X-ray image of Zai's posterior instrumentation and fusion.

Feedback or hardships are not equal to failure. Life rolls on and it has a lot to offer. A setback is a gear change, a brake to take a break from the norm, from the routine, a moment to stop and smell the roses, a moment to take flight and with an eagle's view to relook at life, to redesign and rewrite one's purpose, one's own conviction and existence. Magic happens with heart and action. Zai learnt this through trial and error and discovered that service to mankind is the way to go.

Then in 2007, Zai spotted a demand for fashionable hijabs (veils) for Muslim women and started 'Miztiq Shoppe' through online marketing, which later included men's and children's apparel. In 2012, she had a calling to pursue her Arabic studies and travelled for two years. When she returned to Singapore, she crafted a 'read, write, and speak' Arabic programme, which she taught at Singapore Management University.

In 2014, she discovered business insights and self-discovery lessons coupled with the aid of government support to assist budding entrepreneurs and the present small to medium-sized enterprise to grow their businesses.

She decided to put together her entrepreneurial journey and lessons acquired during her multiple travels to share with the strong-hearted what they can achieve through her experiences. They will be able to swiftly and strategically pursue their passion and turn them into profit almost immediately with little or no money.

Today, Zai Miztiq is a visionary leader, entrepreneur, and CEO of StepUpJourney.com, known for her transformative work in personal and professional development. With over two decades of experience, Zai has empowered individuals across the globe to harness their strengths and passions, turning them into thriving businesses and meaningful life paths.

Her journey is one of resilience and purpose. Zai defied the odds after surviving a near-fatal accident that left her with only a 5% chance of walking again. She not only walked, but she rose—stronger, wiser, and with a mission to uplift others. This extraordinary comeback fuels her teachings on resilience, leadership, and empowerment.

An accomplished author, speaker, and certified Gallup Strengths Coach, Zai is passionate about helping people unlock their potential and live their dreams. Through StepUpJourney.com, she offers a wide range of programmes, from public speaking and leadership coaching to entrepreneurship and corporate social responsibility initiatives. Zai's work is aligned with the UN Sustainable Development Goals, making her a true global advocate for positive change.

Her story is a powerful reminder that with faith, determination, and the right mindset, anyone can transform their life and leave a lasting legacy.

Zai with her role model, best friend, and amazing mother.

Without Motherhood, There is No Prophethood.

Women – they are my role models. My mother was and still is a highly significant, strong, and independent woman figure in my life. Up to this date, I clearly recall how she raised the six of us by herself since dad was mostly not around. Day and night, she fulfilled her duties, both as a father and mother to six mischievous kids. What a tremendous job she did!

Apart from the irreplaceable motherly character, I am also fortunate to have three elder sisters. Two of them got married even before I could spell the word 'aeroplane'. Then there is this one sister that is very dear to me. Our eight-year age gap did not create barriers between us. In fact, we remained so close together and my love for her did not waver. We did many things together, like spending time enjoying the beach and would go cycling together and so much more.

Aside from our weekend activities, we both loved cleaning up the house while blasting Bon Jovi, Debbie Gibson, and Roxette songs out loud. Last but not least, of course, our 'home alone' pastimes were totally enjoyable – we sang aloud, danced to our favourite music, and did some aerobic workouts. It was so much fun!

In addition to this, I have a dad only by name. I never felt a father's love. I only see him performing his prayers and nothing more. I can still recall when he encouraged me to pray. At that time, I did not give any importance to his words as we barely communicated and there was not much connection.

In this fast-paced world where women no longer choose to stay at home, they should be given a chance to explore life and experience economic independence. When a woman has strong faith, becomes financially stable, and is equipped with knowledge to embrace the wisdom of her true being with honour and dignity, this will help eliminate the chance of women being emotionally and spiritually exploited.

In 2014, I started Step Up Journey – a motivational training and coaching consultancy to provide learning solutions to eradicate the struggles of women and youth through education, empowerment, and enrichment programmes for the purpose of standing against bullying and emotional abuse.

It is a prerequisite for peaceful global development that the rights of women are respected. In conflict-ridden areas, in particular, the violation of women leads to the continuation of oppression and suicide from generation to generation.

The objective of this book is to spread the message of love, peace, and freedom. Despite having been through an almost fatal accident that could have led me to paralysis, life goes on. Having picked myself up and established several businesses, I am set to empower, educate, and enrich humanity from all walks of life.

Able or disabled, all of us are unique and wonderful creations of God. It troubles me to read articles about child prostitution and forced marriages just because the family cannot afford to raise the girls. I strongly feel that human empowerment should include women, youth, and men across cultures and communities to be empowered with leadership and entrepreneurial skills. It is essential for humanity to acquire skills and the attitude of being resilient, empathetic, and dynamic in all areas of their lives and work towards enjoying a quality lifestyle while enjoying the process of ageing gracefully and happily.

"Life is too beautiful for you to depend on anyone to make you happy! Choice is yours. Life is short. Live to the fullest!"

The purpose of this book is to eradicate poverty of the pockets and to rewire the poverty of the mind. I believe with the **five Secret Formulas of Success**: Think, Reflect, Understand, Take action, Heal others, readers will be highly inspired and motivated to improve their own situations. I want to inspire you to believe that you can achieve financial independence and to embark on an entrepreneurial journey.

Ladies, a man is not your financial plan! You rule your life and you only live once. It troubles me to hear that many women do not know that they have equal rights and are seen as equal to a man in the eyes of The Almighty God. The Holy Qur'an repeatedly emphasises this equality by addressing both men and women in its verses.

Allah States in the Holy Qur'an:

"But whosoever does good works, whether male or female, and is a believer, such shall enter Heaven, and shall not be wronged even as much as the little hollow in the back of a date stone." (Ch. 4: V. 125)

"And think of the day when thou will see the believing men and the believing women, their light running before them and on their right hands, and it will be said to them, 'Glad tidings for you this day! Gardens through which streams flow, wherein you will abide. That is the supreme triumph'." (Ch. 57: V.13)

"Whoso acts righteously, whether male or female and is a believer, We will surely grant him a pure life; and We will surely bestow on such their reward according to the best of their works." (Ch.16: V.98)

This makes it clear that in Islam, there is equality between men and women. The Prophet Muhammad (peace and blessings be upon him and his family) said: *'It is the duty of every Muslim man and every Muslim woman to acquire knowledge.' (Ibnu Majah)*

Zai Miztiq's Works Since 2001

The above is a brief introduction to the multiple businesses I started and grew over the years. Some are still actively running, while others I had to intentionally let go. It was a tough decision to let go of the 'baby' you have given birth to and have spent a lot of time on. As you read on, I will share how I got started and how you can too.

"Be brave to live the life of your dreams according to your vision instead of the expectations of others."

Photo: *Zai giving an entrepreneurial and motivational talk at Nanyang Polytechnic - a tertiary institution in Singapore.*

Think

Formula #1: Think

There are two types of thinking - regular and critical. The difference between the two is quite profound. For the purpose of our understanding, let's consider one of the definitions provided by *The Foundation for Critical Thinking:*

"Critical thinking is that mode of thinking – about any subject, content, or problem – in which the thinker improves the quality of his or her thinking by skilfully taking charge of the structures inherent in thinking and imposing intellectual standards upon them."

It further states that "Critical thinking is self-guided, self-disciplined thinking which attempts to reason at the highest level of quality in a fair-minded way."

At this stage of the journey, you will explore two main questions:

✓ Who are you?

✓ What do you really want?

Define Yourself

What is your Big Why? What are you an advocate of? Most of the time when faced with this question, people begin to panic. The truth is, do you know what you really want?

Here is a list of questions to think about:

Do you want a better life? Why?

Do you want to travel? Why?

Do you want to be loved and accepted by others? Why?

Do you want to help the poor and feed orphans? Why?

Do you want to pursue higher education, learn, apply, and teach others? Why?

Do you want to make your parents proud? Why?

Do you want your child to respect you as a role model? Why?

Do you have a mess that is a message to serve others? Why?

These are some of the questions that are burning inside you, but you never speak or think seriously about them. Why?

Think About It

"If you don't evolve, you can become extinct!"

Is Starting and Running a Business for You?

The answer is, why not? Many people run away from the idea of entrepreneurship even before they try.

I had someone ask me a question, "Miss Zai, how long is the process to register a company?" I looked at her with a smile and replied, "Three minutes. It is faster than setting up a Facebook account."

I have learnt that sometimes, we are too fearful of the unknown, preferring to stay ignorant. We do not know what we do not know. Are you one of those who prefer to sit and complain about life, cry without a why, finding life boring, and silently hating yourself and those around you? And do you feel that God is utterly unfair? Is that you?

Or on a brighter note, are you seeking to find your calling and your purpose on Earth? And are you seeking ways to be a better person so you can contribute to the community? By contemplating on the above questions, you will have a better understanding of what you truly want. It will also assist you to decide if you wish to be your boss or if you are simply comfortable being employed.

What Your Parents Never Told You

Let me put in simple terms the significant truth your parents never told you.

As an **employee**, there is a boss who takes control of you. You work for others and earn a fixed monthly income no matter how much profit the company you work for gains or not. How much maximum income can you earn? And what if, for any reason, you cannot work anymore?

As a **self-employed** person, you are both the boss and employee. For example, a doctor runs his or her own clinic, and a lawyer runs his or her own law firm.

Being self-employed, you are your own boss. No one can order you around. You work at your own time. Your income depends on the number of hours, amount of investment, and effort you put in. The longer you work, the more you earn, or you may also incur some losses. And what if, for some reason, you become disabled and cannot work anymore?

As a **business owner**, you are the boss. You create employment opportunities for others. You leverage people's time, knowledge, and skills to make money for you.

As an **investor**, money works for you. If you have a huge sum of funds, you make your personal investments, for example, deposit accounts and property, and you generate consistent passive income.

The golden question to ask yourself is, which level are you at and where would you like to be?

Getting Started

The questions that you ask yourself will change your life. To discover your wants, you must first uncover your truth. Before you even begin embarking on the idea of starting to plan an action plan, here are some crucial facts you must dig deep into. Start by confronting the facts. One great CEO began by asking, "Why have we sucked for 100 years?" That's brutal—and it's precisely the type of disciplined question necessary to ignite a transformation. The management climate during a leap from good to great is like a searing scientific debate—with smart, tough-minded people examining hard facts and debating what those facts mean. The point isn't to win the debate, but rather to come up with the best answers, and ultimately, to lock onto a platform that works best.

Face the Facts

Answer these questions honestly, facing the brutal facts without blinking, and you'll begin to see what emerges:

- For new entrepreneurs, why have you not embarked on a business in your lifetime?

- For existing entrepreneurs, why have you not built the business since it was registered?

- What did you do right? What did you do wrong?

- What can you be best at? What can you not be best at?

- What are you and your people deeply passionate about?

- What can you potentially do better than anyone else?

- How can you be a social inventor, designing an environment that would be the seedbed for many insanely great innovations over decades to come?

- How do you focus on building a unique culture that cannot be copied?

- List down ten of your strengths, skills, and talents.

- What makes you truly happy?

- What are your fears and frustrations?

- What are your wants and aspirations?

- How would you serve and add value to your community?

- Who can you work with to guide and mentor you to turn your dreams into reality with confidence and clarity?

*Prophet Muhammad (peace & blessings be upon him & his family)
said, "Seek knowledge even if you have to travel to China."*

Dream It, Achieve It

What are your 101 dreams and goals? The first time I was asked to list this down, I was not able to. It was too much for me. The truth was I had yet to discover what I really wanted. I still had a missing puzzle piece. After attending a series of workshops and seminars, I met a life coach. She sent me a link to do a strengths test and went through the results with me. That was the best test I did in my life. It zoomed in on my natural traits and made me understand and accept myself. It also helped me understand the people around me and bridged the gap between me being a dreamer and a doer. Learning about my innate strengths helped me gain insights into what I can do best naturally. That gave me some sound ideas to confidently implement strategic actions to achieve my goals.

Discovering My Strength

It is truly incumbent on you to spend quality time getting to know yourself and to discover how your unique themes impact your work and personal life. With this knowledge, you can enjoy personal and career success through consistent, near-perfect performance.

Let me share with you my strength finding results and how it benefited me. My signature themes, the ten most dominant, are as follows:

i. Empathy

People who are talented in the Empathy theme can sense the feelings of other people by imagining themselves in others' lives or situations.

ii. Connectedness

People who are talented in the Connectedness theme have faith in the links between all things. They believe there are few coincidences and that almost every event has a reason.

iii. Ideation

People who are talented in the Ideation theme are fascinated by ideas. They are able to find connections between seemingly contrasting phenomena.

iv. Adaptability

People who are talented in the Adaptability theme prefer to 'go with the flow'. They tend to be 'now' people who take things as they come and discover the future one day at a time.

v. Positivity

People who are talented in the positivity theme have an enthusiasm that is contagious. They are upbeat and can get others excited about what they are going to do.

vi. Developer

People who are talented in the Developer theme recognise and cultivate the potential in others. They spot the signs of each small improvement and derive satisfaction from these improvements.

vii. Belief

People who are talented in the belief theme have certain core values that are unchanging. From these values emerges a defined purpose for their life.

viii. Activator

People who are talented in the Activator theme can make things happen by turning thoughts into action.

ix. Maximiser

People who are talented in the Maximiser theme focus on strengths to stimulate personal and group excellence. They seek to transform something strong into something superb.

x. Responsibility

People who are talented in the responsibility theme take psychological ownership of what they say they will do. They are committed to stable values such as honesty and loyalty.

These helped me uncover why I always reacted in certain ways when I hear or witness a situation and why others would react differently. It helped me resolve issues I had with people and I became more accepting as I learnt to better understand them. With this knowledge, it was easier for me to make sound decisions to do what I do best. It's been a magical journey since. And now, as a certified coach, I invite you to discover your strengths and achieve your goals with confidence and clarity with me.

Reflect

Formula #2: Reflect

Imam Hassan (a.s.) said:

"Don't ever regret deep reflection and rationalisation because thinking revives the alert heart and is a key to doors of wisdom."

Zai speaking at The Middle East Show, topic on 'Humanising Events: *How we can include CSR movement in the Industry'*

What is Reflection?

Reflection involves three phases:

1. You have to identify what your mentality and belief system are. What you choose to believe now is an accumulation of your past personal actions, thoughts, and experiences.

2. You have to assess and scrutinise how valid these assumptions are in terms of how they relate to your 'real-life' experience and the present context.

3. You have to transform these assumptions to become more inclusive and integrative and use this new knowledge to bring out the best in you for your future actions and practices.

Here are two examples for you to understand and implement the above. I will describe a scenario and let's observe the general reaction to understand how our human mind is so capable of formulating an assumption and implementing it into our daily lives. These thought processes have been programmed into our core belief system and are constantly backfiring and sabotaging our life's decisions.

Example 1: What are your beliefs about money?

Scenario 1

Descriptive: "I believe that money makes people greedy and selfish."

Analytical: Why? Because, as a child, I was told that although my uncle is a rich man, he never helped my parents when they needed financial support to send me to the best school.

Critical: Now what? After analysing my mindset and belief system about money, I have an alternative perspective and point of view.

Money does not make people greedy and selfish. That is the characteristic of the individual. There are many people who are generous and humble.

Scenario 2

Descriptive: "Money is the root of all evil."

Analytical: Why? Because in almost every TV programme, they portray the rich as scheming and cunning people.

Critical: Now what? Now I understand that money is not evil, people generally are.

Scenario 3

Descriptive: "Money cannot buy happiness."

Analytical: Why? Even though the superstars are rich and famous, they are unhappy and have to turn to substance addictions like drugs and alcohol. Eventually, they fall into depression and commit suicide.

Critical: Now what? I know that when I gain riches and abundance, I have the freedom to choose my desired lifestyle, and buy gifts and travel with my loved ones.

Trip to the Maldives with mummy.

Without money and willpower, I would never have been able to achieve this priceless moment.

Example 2: What are the fears you have?

Each one of us has our own fears. Here are 12 of the top known fears for you to address:

i.   Fear of Rejection

ii. Fear of Change

iii. Fear of Failure

iv. Fear of Poverty

v.   Fear of Criticism

vi. Fear of Ill Health

vii. Fear of Loss

viii. Fear of Success

ix. Fear of Being Alone

x.   Fear of Old Age

xi. Fear of Death

xii. Fear of Having Wealth

Here, we will describe the scenario and observe the general reaction and how we can switch the distorted programming.

Scenario 1

Descriptive: "I fear rejection"

Analytical: Why? Because I was once rejected when I met a potential client, and he chased me out of the house!

But after analysing my thoughts, I have an alternative perspective and point of view on this fear.

Critical: Now what? Just because one client rejected my business, I should not be affected by that past. I have had ninety-nine other clients who accepted my idea and were happy to buy from me.

Scenario 2

Descriptive: "I fear criticism"

Analytical: Why? Because, when I was young, I thought I did the best project work in school, but the teacher and all the students criticised my work, and my teacher threw the project work out of the classroom.

Critical: Now what? Just because the teacher and the students did not like my project work, so what? Today, I am running a business and generating profits from the very same idea from the school assignment.

Scenario 3

Descriptive: What? "I fear failure"

Analytical: Why? What if? I once brought back home a report book with a single red line. I failed Math, and my dad hit me so hard that it left my right cheek with his fingerprints.

Critical: Now what? After analysing my thoughts, I have an alternative perspective and point of view about this fear. It was a blessing in disguise that my dad hit me. After that incident, I never scored below 70% in Mathematics.

The exercise above is meant to help you uncover the root cause of your past pain and for you to acknowledge that your existing unnecessary emotions are no longer serving you. As your coach and guide, it is my task to facilitate you to gain new insights in all areas of your life and to help you see the light at the end of the tunnel.

"Face your fear and watch it disappear."

"Are you ready to step up and bring out the resilient, confident, and compassionate human leader in you?"

Mastering the Negative

Only you have the power to turn your life around. I clearly recall an event that happened when I was nine.

My mother was called to school to collect my end of year report book. At the end of the Parent-Teacher conference, my teacher said six words to my mum.

And these words kept lingering in my head until they got embedded in my heart. He said, "Your daughter is a slow coach." I still recall his voice as I pen this down. Now when I reflect back, I question myself, am I really slow? And if I am, so what? Slow and steady wins the race.

Easier said than done, you may say. It's not easy to erase painful memories, especially when such words come from people you respect and love. It might have been true or he may be wrong. However, in the present moment, it is not useful. I am not who or what I used to be. Even if I am still the same, I know I have the power and capability to make a change. The point is, do I want to make a change and step up? Also, the best gift I have learnt is to see your weakness as a blessing to help others.

"It is not where you are, but who you aspire to be."
Speaking in Riyadh, Saudi Arabia about 'Financial Independence' with empowered women leaders from around the world!

Turning your Life Around

I felt like a total failure after the accident of 2005 where I was left almost paralysed. I was on self-controlled morphine and had to depend on medical drugs to assist my mobility. I felt that I was doomed and done. There was no turning back. There goes my dream of setting up my henna art academy in Japan and around the world. There goes my life. I will never be the doting and dutiful daughter I always dreamed of being.

Bouncing Back with Self-Encouragement

I still recall the first time I visited my physiotherapist, two weeks after being in the hospital ward. Transported in a wheelchair like a slouched, spineless body to the physiotherapy clinic, I had no strength to even sit up straight.

The next moment, the doctor told me to stand up on my feet. I had difficulty and was aided by three nurses. And then, just when I thought I had experienced the worst, I was asked to walk, to take a step forward. I jammed. I could not move.

The honest truth was, I did not know how to do it. I could not lift my feet. Then, one of the nurses whispered to me, "You walk with your hips." At that moment, it felt like an angel's whisper. I just wanted to cry. All my life, I took for granted the ability to move my hips and strode arrogantly with each step on Earth without giving thanks to my creator for the ability to walk. Wow!

I maintained my composure. I attempted a five-minute walking exercise, and I could not get through it. I was so thwarted that I failed. Little did I see that there was wisdom in the tragedy. I was about to go through a massive learning curve to master how to turn my pain into power. A blessing in disguise, today, I am invited to speak at world-class events to inspire and move hearts.

Zai at a UN simulation event in Dubai addressing diplomats and world leaders about 'Effective Communication & Collaboration Skills'

Where the Miracle Begins

It has been almost a year since the accident. Doctors had claimed that I would be left with chronic disabling pain for the rest of my life. I lived a dreadful and clueless life. Seriously, I did not know what to do and what was coming. The only thing I did was, I whined on and on about being a victim. Then one morning, a miracle happened. I was inspired to do some volunteer work to feel useful again.

Despite the broken spine, I was yearning and dreaming of doing volunteer work overseas. I did some research online and took the first step to visit a local charity organisation. I told them I had time and wanted to contribute to the community. I then wrote to a youth group and spent some time with them on a short-term project. At that moment, I was unaware that I was silently weakening the enemies within me that had been nurturing me to whine and complain about life. As I increased my resilience to do something worthy with my time, I began to feel good within. This enabled me to end my procrastination. It lifted my spirit, and I seized the moment deciding to soar higher. I was determined to do my best.

Doing the Remarkable

A mantra I live by, "It is up to you to be a victim or be victorious. You may have a physical disability, but you are still gifted with a sound mind and a strong, loving heart to take action. Give thanks for life, help yourself and move on to help others." And certainly, if you believe in the power of God, His Abundance is Limitless. You have been created for a purpose. Your job is to do your best, and God will do the rest.

Zai conducting a youth training in Singapore
"Brave Leadership – Be a warrior, not a worrier"

Arm yourself with love and confidence and set out to do what you love, loving what you do strategically. This will keep you feeling wholesome and happy. I did it, and so can you!

Arm Yourself with Confidence

Before I became a global speaker, I used to attend many conferences and events. I once attended an all-ladies conference filled with five hundred participants. The line-up of speakers was life coaches, motivators, and image consultants promising to empower women. It was fun and hyped up at the beginning. However, at the end, I realised that many women were rushing to sign up for programmes because they had low self-esteem and major self-image issues. They needed to seek validation and approval from an external source to feel 'good enough and accepted'. The moment I discovered this, I knew there was more to be done to support humanity to step up. I wanted to impart knowledge and skills on how one can gain confidence and self-acceptance through an inner-healing transformation.

What is your definition of being confident? An individual who is highly dependent on Botox injections and multiple plastic surgeries, dressed in revealing clothes, loaded with tonnes of makeup on the face and flashing her $10,000 Prada shoes. Is that confidence?

My personal outlook to thrive harmoniously in this world is to balance being modest and still maintaining confidence. It may sound ironic. How will a person remain humble yet buoyantly uphold a poise of self-assurance? Let me share with you how.

Confidence of Superiority

vs.

Confidence of Humility

In my opinion, there are two categories of being confident. The first is confidence of superiority. This is usually built upon a foundation of someone who has multiple issues and insecurities. They constantly feel inferior to others no matter what level they are at. To cover up their fake confidence, they seek temporary relief to feel or look good. Most times, these people find a great need to put others down, almost causing destruction to others. They find joy in doing this solely to experience personal elevation.

Confidence of humility, on the other hand, can only be exuded by being authentic. You are self-sufficient, self-assured, and have no hidden agenda of any sort to benefit from others. You become a natural communicator and connect with people tactfully, experiencing beautiful in-the-moment energy exchange. You carry yourself well, and you influence people with your sincerity, positivity, and love. You spontaneously become a people magnet.

At this stage, it is important for you to do a personal audit to determine which group you belong to. The first group or the latter? Whichever you decide, we know that nobody is perfect. We are all learning and growing every day.

"An inner-healing transformation journey will help you evolve and bring out the resilient, confident, compassionate leader in you." – Zai Miztiq

The real beauty is to be confident and put full trust in the realm of God's Divinity. When you are ready to let go and let God, you will attain a magical level of confidence. Nothing will hold you back. You become light.

What would you do if you Weren't Afraid?

Firstly, you have to delete the distorted past programming that has taught you to be obedient and to remain quiet - silencing your voice and suppressing your opinions, fearing you will come across as rude, stupid, or trying to be too smart.

If you could live your life anew, what would you do differently? What change would radiate from within you?

Actively count on yourself as you are your best companion to succeed. Only you can make yourself happy! And only you can decide for yourself and choose to be who you want to be. Life is not about whining but shining. The magic tip is to survive and thrive with flexibility and look within yourself.

The Magic Is in You.

You Only Live Once

Ideas can make money. What are your dreams and goals? When you know what you want, and why you want it, the how will follow through!

Putting it Down on Paper

When you know what you want, only then can you visualise it. Think about it, "If you can't even attempt to write down your goals, how will you be able to take massive action to achieve it?" So to make it easy, let's break down the goals into nine priorities of life. Then under each heading, break it down further to specify your goals and write it down as if it has already taken place.

"Redesign & rewrite your life. You only live once."

Be Specific! Know What you Want

THE NINE GOALS

1. Hereafter, goals

2. Personal goals

3. Family goals

4. Business goals

5. Financial goals

6. Health goals

7. Social goals

8. Education goals

9. Travel goals

Example: Business Goal

I own an active online web portal, www.stepupjourney.com that serves individuals who are frustrated with life and are seeking motivation to take purposeful action. I have in place the best quality books, online masterclasses, and coaching programmes – empowering one million global clients by 22nd April 2025.

Example: Travel Goal

"In September 2026, I am on The Caribbean Islands with my siblings, having breakfast in our water villa being served by a good-looking service-oriented butler."

The magic word is 'BE SPECIFIC!'

A Challenge to Grow

Believe it or not, in life, you are your own biggest enemy. Who sabotaged your personal success? Who is the one with the limiting self-belief? And who is stopping you from turning your dreams into reality? Stop hiding behind the veils and start showing up for yourself.

"To move forward, you must first take a step" - Chase S.

Understand

Formula #3: Understand

"Seek knowledge from the womb to the tomb"
My graduation from the Psychotherapy and Counselling programme

Take a pause from your routine and set out to seek knowledge. You will be amazed at what you will discover.

Taking Care of the Temple

"As a good wine must be kept in a good cask, so a wholesome body is the proper foundation for a well-appointed inner ground." – Johannes Tauler

It is essential that you stay true to your underlying principles and remain transparent to yourself. Understand your Brand DNA. Be on truth and work on your mission. Understand the fine line of difference between the ability to adapt and to compromise on what you stand for. Never succumb to the words of people and go against your heart. Think with your heart and act with your head.

Appreciate yourself and know that you are a wonderful and unique creation of God. You have the right to seize your God-given birthright to succeed with honour and dignity. What God intended for you goes far beyond anything you can imagine. Hang on to the rope of your Creator, and you shall not fail or falter. And most importantly, health is wealth. Prioritise your well-being. You become what you eat. Be mindful of your dietary intake, quality of sleep, and keep up with an exercise routine.

Contentment vs. Laziness

For many years, I ran a small enterprise. It was fun. I did what I loved. I travelled whenever and wherever I would like to visit. I served whichever client I liked. Pretty much, I was contented working from home as an online seller. On average, I made about $5,000 a month. Since the beginning of 2014, I looked at my income and asked myself if I still wanted to earn only that amount. Is there anything else I could do?

Then an unexpected email came. It was from a friend who does fundraising for her intensive community work in China. They were raising $60,000 to build schools and learning centres. I was eager to help without delay. Three days after I posted a few messages on Facebook, I raised

$1,500. Then a voice came to me, "When are you going to write a $10,000 cheque for charity?"

I never thought of it. But it was a great wake-up call. I had been too complacent in my comfort zone. I needed to upgrade my knowledge and skills. I knew deep in my heart I wanted to understand people and help them. There are too many people who are depressed - exhausted from work and family. And there are many who are tired of living and toying with suicidal thoughts. I knew it was time for me to step up and do something greater.

The Little Voice

I learnt about the little voices that like to tell me, "You can't do it! You are not good enough! Why you? You are not meant for success. You are too lazy, forget it and just take a chill pill!"

Yes, you have little voices. But so what? Tell him/her, "Thank you very much for your feedback. Feedback does not mean failure. I am better than what you think of me. Now get out of my head!"

Success can be Easy

Being successful in business or life is not by sheer luck. It is about acquiring knowledge and taking strategic massive action.

Being the Makeup Artist President of Nanyang Polytechnic's Makeup Artist Club was a very memorable and fruitful experience. During those times, I would rather die than leave home without applying makeup, especially my liquid eyeliner. In 2005, when I was still modelling, I was asked to be a face model for a makeup book authored by a celebrity from Singapore.

After the photo shoot, I had the chance to look through the digital photos and strangely noticed that I felt more beautiful and confident in the pre-makeup shots compared to the after makeup photos. I loved my natural look more even though their makeup work was excellent. At that very moment, I understood the quote, "Beauty is but skin deep." It was the beginning of my journey to master what true beauty meant. Along the way, I learnt that "It is not the fake superficial makeup that will grant you success, but what comes from within."

"Where your attention goes, your time goes" – Idawo K

Tips to Speed up your Way to Wealth

These are some of the pointers you need to understand as you embark on a lucrative and successful entrepreneurial journey.

1. **Influencing Power:** To inspire people, speak from the heart.

2. **Centre of Influence:** It's not just what you know, but who you know.

3. **Branding Power:** Be the brand that people want to associate with.

4. **Social Media Marketing:** The best marketing tool, and it is free!

5. **Client Attraction:** Learn the essentials of gaining attention and attracting people with what you can offer that is beneficial to them.

6. **Cash is Power:** Monetise your talents and turn it into profit.

Stay Positive All the Way

Another way to stay focused and consistently motivated to work on your dreams is to surround yourself with a network of goal-getters. Your environment, choice of words, and thought process determine your success and how quickly you will get there.

Avoid spending time with those who zap your energy and pull you down. If you are certain you are on the right path, attain the right tools and mindset and just go for it. Trying to explain yourself to someone who will never get your point is super exhausting and may unnecessarily put doubts in you.

Power of Gratitude and Prayers

Practice writing down at least ten things that you are thankful for daily. Pray! Pray and continuously ask God to keep you steadfast on the right path. One of my most favourite and powerful prayers that keeps me going is this, **"Dear Lord, melt me, mould me, fill me and use me purposefully."**

You will experience an amazing miracle of how things will unfold. Give thanks to The Almighty and ask Him to guide you and let Him use you to be the vehicle to guide others to Him. Ameen.

Take Action

Formula #4: Take Action

The Prophet Muhammad (peace and blessings be upon him and his family) said: "If anyone travels on a road in search of knowledge, God will cause him to travel on one of the roads of Paradise."

The Power of Ideas

Ideas. They are very powerful. Sometimes the worst of ideas are the best of money makers. Many people I have spoken to tell me, "Zai, I want to do business, but I have no idea what I want to sell." I believe many of you can relate to that.

For me, I never had the mindset that I am selling something to someone. I always share what I see is a need for me, believing it could be a need for another as well. When I spot a product or service that can benefit others, I will do my research to learn briefly about it, acquire it and start sharing with others.

An example would be how I started my online hijab business. In 2007, I started donning the hijab. To get started was almost impossible. I was a model. I used to have a dress code to kill. Now I decided to be all covered up. What was I thinking? But it was a spiritual calling, and I thank God I followed the call.

So I brought $200 to town to find something that would look nice yet modest. I personally am not a shopaholic.

I know what I want and would walk into a store to get it. However, there was a huge problem. After the 129th store, I still did not find a suitable modest fashion apparel that would match my style.

The same year, I took a forty-day London-Cyprus-Syria trip with my niece. On that journey, I met a lot of ladies in hijab and observed what was trending and in style. In Syria, I discovered the Al-Hamidiyy souk. It was a treasure hunt. I found lots of beautiful scarves, accessories, and dresses and was shopping for some friends back home. Being the enterprising me, what cost £30 was sold at a higher price. At that time, I had no thought of running a hijab business. All that mattered to me was at least to get my flights paid for. And yes, it did.

Upon my return, since I bought extra shopping items, I took photos of them and posted them on Facebook. I introduced nine colours of the inner scarf which I found to be very comfortable compared to what we have back home. I felt like I found the most innovative and cool product to serve the ladies. The ones I had bought before were all too tight or caused so much pain in my ear that would lead me to having migraines.

Dear readers, read between the lines. I had a need. I could not find it in my community. I travelled and found an item that would save me from killer migraines. I wanted to serve the community with something cool and innovative which I eventually discovered. Three minutes after my first FB post, I had my first five orders. I just made my first £25. After a week, I sold out my 120 pieces of stock.

So, what did I do with my earnings? Did I spend it away? No. It was a capital start-up for me. With the capital, I ordered more stocks. Starting from nine colours, Miztiq Shoppe had a collection of ninety colours. Gradually, I added shawls, dresses, arm gloves, and brooches upon customers' request.

Miztiq Shoppe started in 2008 and has delivered orders within Singapore and even up to the British Virgin Islands, The Caribbean. I was happily making sales and happier to know that God has used me as a tool to encourage many women and girls from different walks of life to start donning the hijab.

Many of us have a multi-million-dollar money-making idea. But how do we fully utilise it? To me, ideas are the inspiration of God and the whispers of angels. The very least we can do is to attempt it. If you think you cannot, at least share it with someone who can plant the seed and nurture the idea to grow into something beneficial. I do believe that what goes around comes around. If you do not benefit from the sharing financially, you will receive rewards in other forms, in forms you can never imagine. Have faith and have compassion for humankind. But do also watch out for your rice bowl and protect it. Do understand that benevolence does not equate to stupidity.

Searching for Information

Citing the above example, I am certain some of you are going to give an excuse that not all of us are gifted to travel to find a product to share with people.

Having gone through a real-life experience, I can safely guarantee you that if you make the right intention and take action, miracles will inevitably appear. With the highly advanced technology we have today, there is no excuse that you cannot find something to do or sell to serve and add value to others. With social media and viral marketing, this is the best era for mankind to set upon a successful and lucrative entrepreneurial journey. Always be on a constant search for knowledge. Take breaks in between to smell the roses. Ideas and inspiration come to me best when I am travelling. Travelling enables the recharging of the mental and spiritual batteries. And when you learn new things and apply them to your life, you can then move forward to teach them to others.

Blessed are those who Learn and Impart it to Others

'Read-Write-Speak Arabic' is a 7-level training programme that I designed after my return from a two-year Arabic learning expedition. Starting from Jordan, I travelled to Morocco and then I journeyed to Tarim, Yemen. How did the idea of drawing up a lesson come about?

Two years before I travelled, I attempted to learn the Arabic language from a few teachers in Singapore. I found it really difficult to learn the language.

Even though I grasped something, I realised that I had no one to practise with in my home country. I knew it was impossible to master a language by only spending two hours a week in a classroom setting.

At the same time, I reflected, why was it that when I was living in Japan, doing and teaching henna art, I could master the Japanese language in less than a month? I was able to communicate with the Japanese people as though I knew the language from before.

"A girl's gotta do, what a girl's gotta do!"

I then decided to travel to Jordan for an Arabic immersion programme to fulfil my learning goals. I still recall my first day of school. My teacher, Mr. Mahmood, was a native Arabic speaker. He did not speak a word of English at all. Learning a foreign language is not easy. Every single day, I would cry and pray that God would make it easy for me so that I could teach it to others back home. And truly, my dream came true.

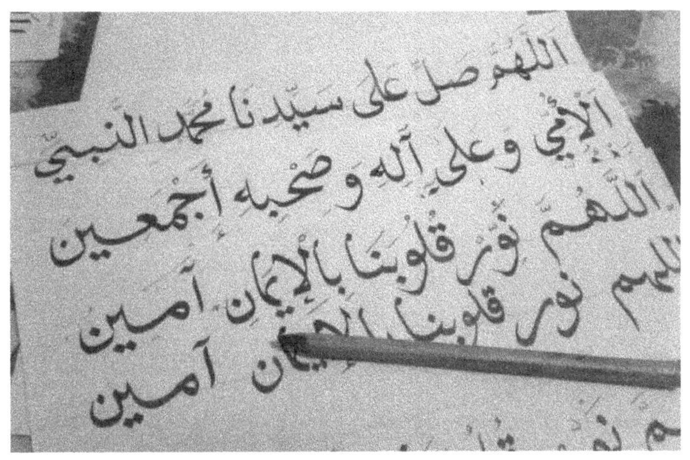

Zai's first few attempts at Arabic Calligraphy

I returned to Singapore in early January 2014. A month later, I received a call from a local university to teach 'Arabic for Business Conversation' to their students. I was ecstatic about the blessed opportunity. I enthusiastically customised and prepared a lesson plan to meet my learners' profile.

My first batch of 'Arabic for Business Conversation' training programme for the students of Singapore Management University.

Just when I thought the best had already happened, on 22nd April 2014, there was a full-page write-up by 'Berita Harian', a local newspaper featuring the story of my Arabic learning adventures, the struggles, and the multiple blessings. It is incumbent on us to invest time, money, and effort to seek knowledge. And it is highly recommended that we spread the knowledge we have acquired with the intention of reaping worthy rewards for our Hereafter.

In my aspiration to serve others, I was granted a priceless opportunity to do Arabic to English translation for Channel News Asia, Singapore. My future plan is to work with some masters of the Arabic language to develop software for the seven levels of my read-write-speak Arabic training programme in a book and digital format.

Zero your Cup

This was the first lesson I learnt when I was searching for a business guide. I was introduced to a business coach whom I had seen on Facebook claiming that she earns $50,000 a month. I was wondering if this was for real and had doubts about it.

One fine day, I was invited to her event. Despite being sceptical, I said to myself, I have nothing to lose, let's give it a shot. As I sat at the preview, all the monkey chatter in my head was telling me this is a scam and I should not even be there wasting my time.

To kill the chatter, I said to it, "I am earning £5,000 a month through Facebook marketing. I want to learn how this lady earns £50,000 a month. So please go away." Surprisingly, it worked.

The first lesson presented was to 'Zero Your Cup'. If we do not empty a filled cup, how will we fill it with new and beneficial substances?

"Your energy is your greatest asset – make sure to replenish yourself
before giving to others."
– Zai Miztiq

Plan the Act & Act the Plan

1. Attending training is the first step. Learning from those who have gone through years of 'hard knocks' helps to accelerate your growth.

2. Applying what was taught is the next step. Any knowledge without action is fruitless.

3. It is important for you to stay connected with a mastermind group as it helps you align with your plans and goals.

It is not going to be easy and all glamorous at first, but with consistency and hard work, all will be well. Keep walking! It is going to be worth it if you live your dreams and strive for what you believe in!

Increasing your Value to the Marketplace

I have heard from way too many people how they are uncomfortable with the idea of selling things and that doing business is not their forte. To overcome the above ordeal, first, find the need and identify how you can add value to others. Many people do not like the word business because they associate business people with a conman. Add value to the marketplace. Be useful to others. Serve and make a difference. Be the trusted name.

Generating Creative Ideas

Miztiq Henna & Body Art was born in December 2001. The most popular interview question is, "How did I embark on my henna art journey?" One fine evening, my cousin paid me a visit. She brought henna paste and some design books.

The only thing I clearly remember was her saying, "Zai, please draw henna for me. I am attending a wedding this weekend and I think you have the talent to draw." Unwaveringly, I just smiled and started drawing on her hands and palm. To be honest, since young, I am passionate about henna and always had it adorned on me. I never dreamed I would pick up a cone to draw it for someone.

The lesson here is that, **never say no to an opportunity that appears before you**. Someone brought you the supplies and was 120% confident in you. There is nothing to lose. **Just do it.**

"When you work for money, people run from you. When you work to serve people, money runs to you!" – Zai Miztiq

After an hour of drawing, my cousin was delighted and even tipped me. I never intended then to turn my passion into profit. I was just happy doing it, even if I did not get paid. The more I drew, the better I got at it. During the same period, since I was the President of the Makeup Artist Club in my school, I introduced henna art to the team. Ever since then, we always did henna art for school events. I later discovered I was interested in other forms of body painting works as well. I became so popular in henna with the girls at school that even their family members started contacting me for it. Then, one of them started enquiring about bridal henna. I had a friend who was working for an events company, and they were looking for henna artists and face painters. I instantaneously headed a team of talents for private and corporate events. I was creating job opportunities and grew a source of income. A month later, a friend designed my business card, and the rest was history. I became known for being a talent management company, and the business grew through a very strong word-of-mouth advertising.

As months passed, new services were included in the talents list, for example, nail art and rice art jewellery making. Then we introduced latte art where a professional barista would set up a mobile coffee station, serving guests specialty coffee topped with a customised logo - a great marketing tool for businesses. Then I noticed that mobile photo booths were trending. Seeing an opportunity, I incorporated it into our events to inject fun and creativity at events and parties.

Tap on What is Trending

"Henna art demo at a cake factory in Sibiu, Romania."

To be innovative, you have to think out of the box on how you can maximise your talents. Let me give you an example. When cake baking was trending, how can henna art tap on the riding wave? I started experimenting drawing henna art designs on cakes and cookies.

A new creation of Henna Art on Cookies for a kids' party

When I launched my henna art on cake idea during one of the festive seasons, I was interviewed on TV. Through the media publicity, I had many bakers request to participate in my training programme, 'Get Creative & Innovative with Henna Art'.

The Power of Personal Branding

Zai Miztiq spent nearly a year doing therapy and back-strengthening treatments to learn to walk again. (Photo: Zai Miztiq)

Media appearances can be quite contagious. First the radio, then the magazine, then the national newspapers, and you swiftly qualify to be a celebrity public figure. Once you get featured, you keep getting spotted locally and internationally. Personal branding helps with influencing people and eases your communication and relationship building. It supports you to execute ideas with less speech and more purposeful action.

When Life Gives you Lemons, Make Lemonade

In 2003, I wanted to travel to Japan to spread my love for henna. I recall casually writing down my mission statement. "Our mission is to travel the world with henna art to inspire people and spread the beauty of the traditional Indian art to as many people as possible from all corners of the world."

With so much zeal and excitement, I was quite taken aback by something one of my family members said just a day before I flew off. She made a passing remark to my mum: "Can't you afford to raise Zai up that she has to wander so far away from you to make a living?"

And she turned to me and said, "And you, why do you have to do a $5 business? We are all well-off. We have assets worth half a million dollars. What can your $5 business do for you?"

That was a powerful statement. Since then, I never turned back. I stayed true to my passion. I knew I was in for something BIG. I did not know what, but I knew something big was coming. Those words became a solid foundation and affirmed my decision. I arrived in Japan on the 5th of March 2003, in the heart of the bitter cold winter. There was no way I could sit and do henna on the streets of Shibuya or Harajuku and attempt to make money. I did try. But the torturous weather brawled with me. I really thought I was going to freeze to death on the streets. So, did I fly back? No way! I kept asking God to show me a way. Why was I in Japan? What else can I do? What are the opportunities available for me to demonstrate my henna art?

There were tonnes of questions that kept coming to me, and I used my **Formula of T.R.U.T.H.** to solve my problem.

1. I started **thinking** and **reflecting** on what brought me to Japan?

2. Then I **understood** my purpose. I gathered information from the locals that many people organised indoor gatherings and enjoyed participating in hobby craft activities during the colder season.

3. I **took action** by writing to the media to make them aware of my presence in Japan and that I would like to share my Indian cultural art to their audience. I

received free publicity. Thanks to the article, event organisers and party planners started to contact me to do henna art at their parties. Through the parties, I met many new friends who later became my henna art students.

4. And through imparting my knowledge, many of my students, in turn, worked closely with us at events, earning a side income. And after I left Japan, my students benefited from henna and are still doing it until today.

My first live radio interview in Japan at Tokyo FM radio station

Creating Opportunity

It has been a fruitful experience for me since I embarked on my mission to spread henna art in and outside of Singapore. Not only did I earn money from it, but I also gained many friends who eventually became family. From being a henna art customer, some of them are now professional henna artists, and a few of them are Miztiq's henna art trainers.

Can you imagine that you too can create career opportunities from a very simple idea? In whatever you do, always draw up a clear roadmap of where you can take your ideas. Nothing is impossible.

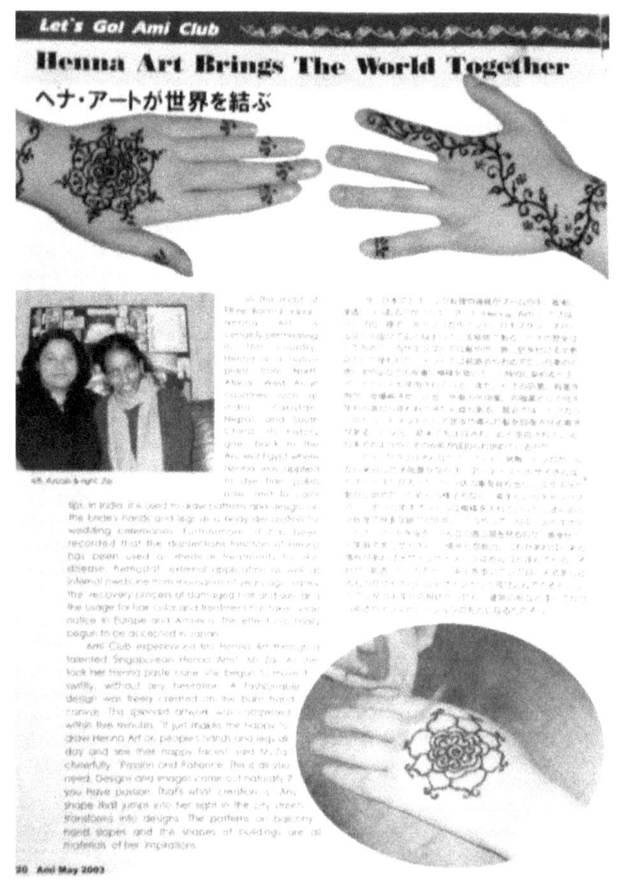

An interview and feature of 'Miztiq Art' in Tokyo, Japan.

Taking your Passion and Skills to the Next Level

Amid running the 'Step Up' motivational workshops and leading my 'Sisterhood Mentorship Programme,' I've also created the 'Learn to Earn with Henna Art' educational video series. This initiative is designed to empower individuals with a valuable life skill that can provide them with financial independence for a lifetime.

Henna art has been my passion for years, and now I'm intentionally taking it to new heights. Drawing from my experience of serving thousands of clients since 2001, this video series is my way of sharing that knowledge and enriching lives across the globe, all while embracing the opportunities of the digital age.

My hope is that, whether I'm here or not, as long as technology and the internet exist, these tools and training videos will continue to empower and inspire others. This is my dream—my legacy. Now, I ask you: What dreams are you ready to pursue? What legacy will you leave behind?

Zai on the set of 'Learn to Earn with Henna Art' production

Developing your Craft

I have many more dreams in my pipeline, and one of them is to develop a systematic franchise plan to bring henna and body art to a global stage. This will not only showcase a beautiful cultural tradition but also create a platform for economic empowerment opportunities worldwide.

As you embark on your own journey to live your dreams and leave a lasting legacy, always remember to uplift the disabled and less fortunate. Seek out ways to be more inclusive in everything you do.

Thinking Beyond the Norm: Empowering Through Social Responsibility

As you journey through this book, you may find that turning your passion into profit isn't just about personal success—it's about making a meaningful contribution to the world. Thinking outside the box allows us to explore new avenues for impact and innovation. At Step Up Journey, we believe in creating pathways that not only uplift individuals but also empower communities.

Step Up Journey launches Braille Edition of Amazon Bestseller, empowering the visually impaired worldwide. – The UAE Daily

In March 2024, we proudly launched the Braille edition of '**Turn Your Passion into Profit**', an initiative designed to empower the visually impaired globally. This project was made possible through the generous support of **SK**

Dazzle DMCC, one of our trusted corporate partners, as part of their **Corporate Social Responsibility (CSR)** initiative. Their commitment to supporting educational empowerment through Step Up Journey's **Community Solutions Programme** aligns with the **UN Sustainable Development Goals**, proving that organisations can enhance their brand while creating lasting, positive change.

Through these initiatives, we invite organisations to think differently – by not only meeting their corporate objectives but also contributing to the betterment of society. If you are part of an organisation with a CSR department or simply looking for ways to make a difference, consider how you can join us in creating empowered, inclusive communities. Together, we can transform lives while building a lasting legacy.

Step Up Journey launches Braille Edition of Turn Your Passion into Profit with team SK Dazzle DMCC

How to Stay at the Top of the Game?

From being an individual online seller, I directly moved on to encouraging others to embark on a lucrative home-based online business. Seeing how genuine and generous I am in teaching them, some of them became my resellers. And to further assist my resellers with their new-found business, I impart my personal branding knowledge, sales and marketing skills, and I heavily emphasise providing service beyond excellence.

A long time ago, during the school holidays, I worked with Disney when they had a 'DisneyFest' event in Singapore. I was 17 then. After a few weeks at work, we were notified there would be a service excellence award given out. I had no clue I was a nominee. And when they announced the result, my name was called. I was amazed. I later asked my supervisor how I got the award. He said the top management was observing me. I did not understand.

Then slowly, I got more information and understood the importance of being service-oriented in all that you do to stay ahead of the game.

Going the extra mile, especially when you run an online business, matters because the customers do not see you, yet they trust you enough to buy from you.

How do we present and be at the top of the game when you are an online seller? Packaging matters. How you assist the customers in their buying decisions matters. And the after-sales service also matters.

An example of going the extra mile would be when we know a customer is buying a gift for his/her family member or friend, ask them if they would like you to add a note to the gift, or even offer to gift-wrap the products and have it hand-delivered to the gift recipient. This may seem like a hassle, but be comfortable with the idea and disseminate it well. It will go a long way.

When you are an online seller, it means your shoppers are seeking efficiency, ease, and convenience. Be the solution provider. Educate and entertain your customers about your latest arrivals. You are sharing about a product and selling it to the emotions of your buyers. Who are you targeting? Why do they need it? How will it benefit the end users? What will the community gain from this effort?

To impart my business skills and knowledge that I have shared so far in my book, I have produced a masterclass for you to learn how you can step-by-step get started on turning your passion into profit. To gain access to my class, visit www.stepupjourney.com

Travel Is in My DNA

Over the years, I have visited more than thirty-four countries, immersed in different cultures and gained many international friends. The beauty of travelling is that it rejuvenates your mind, body and soul. When you make time to stride humbly to witness the beauty of the world, every step will enable you to come back to a full circle of finding yourself.

In 2010, I made an intention to travel to seek or impart knowledge. Since then, I have been blessed to begin my career as a global speaker and travelling trainer. As I continuously travel, my vision became clearer to embark on a 'Step Up Journey' to empower, educate, and enrich lives.

An opportunity to give a motivational talk at an orphanage while on my travels in Kashmir, India

Do it Right, Right Away

There is truly no rocket science formula for starting and running a business. The secret is, **there is no secret**. Do not wait on people or seek validation. It is about discovering your passion and believing in your idea. Then swiftly take strategic actions and know that you are born awesome and can achieve anything you put your heart to. What usually would stop you from succeeding is when you over-analyse until you become paralysed. It is great to think and to make informed choices. But thinking too much will lead to procrastination, killing the magic and motivation. Go with the flow with knowledge, strategy and a proper system and you will go a long way. To get to your goal, you must take the first step first. In the event you start feeling demotivated and need a gentle reminder to push through, remember this, "What material success does is to provide you with the ability to concentrate on things that really matter. And that will not only make a difference in your own life, but in the lives of others."

"A guide can walk you to the door, but you must choose to walk through it."

Heal Others

Formula #5: Heal Others

God Is Aware of the Good Things That You Do

"They ask you (O Muhammad) what they should spend in charity. Say: 'Whatever you spend with a good heart, give it to parents, relatives, orphans, the helpless, and travellers in need. Whatever good you do, God is aware of it.'"

The Holy Quran, 2:215

Re-find and Refine your Philosophy of Life

The key to victory is to have the end in mind. When we have a vision, it helps us embark on a purposeful mission. As for me, one of my biggest passions is to learn and teach. I love to share beneficial knowledge in the hope of helping and uplifting others.

The Prophet (peace and blessings be upon him and his family) said, "When a man dies, his deeds come to an end except for three: A continuous charity, knowledge by which people derive benefit, and a pious child who prays for him." *(Sahih Muslim)*

"The wound is the place where the light enters you."
- Mawlana Rumi

Life Goes On

If I had a guidebook like this to give me hope after my near-death experience, it would have made all the difference. I vividly remember how each visit to the doctor or therapist felt like an overwhelming burden. I would leave the hospital feeling lost, uncertain, and completely helpless.

The fear of not knowing what the future held, of not seeing any light at the end of the tunnel, was devastating.

Though my broken spine was slowly healing, it took nearly two years for my spirit to gather the strength to rise again. I was burdened by a fractured belief system and constantly feared whether I could navigate the world with a permanent disability. I longed for a role model—someone who could offer me hope and guidance, someone to help me rebuild my confidence and find meaning again.

Now that I've found my strength, I want you to find yours. Life is beautiful, and every new day is a second chance. If I can rise from the ashes of despair, so can you. Have hope—because your journey is far from over. Your STEP UP JOURNEY is only getting started!

What is Holistic Healing?

Holistic healing takes a comprehensive approach to wellness, focusing not only on treating physical symptoms but also addressing the mind, body, and spirit as interconnected parts of a whole. It is about consciously living a balanced lifestyle, rather than seeking quick fixes for health issues. This form of healing encourages an ongoing journey of personal discovery, self-development, and the pursuit of wholeness, aiming to create lasting harmony in all areas of life.

As you embark on your journey of self-discovery, you are making an informed choice to refine your state of being—body, mind, and soul. With growth comes a natural desire to uplift others as well. To play the role of a healer in your community, it is essential to cultivate specific traits and values, such as:

1. THE POWER OF CONTRIBUTION

The Prophet Muhammad (peace and blessings be upon him) said, "Charity is prescribed for every descendant of Adam, every day the sun rises." When asked what form this charity should take, he responded, "The doors of goodness are many… enjoining good, removing harm, guiding those in need, supporting the weak, and even smiling at your brother is charity." (Fiqh-us-Sunnah, Volume 3, Number 98).

True healing begins when we contribute to the well-being of others, whether through small acts of kindness or by being present in times of need.

2. THE POWER OF GRATITUDE

Learning to say 'Thank you'—both to those who help us and those who challenge us—can transform the heart. Gratitude dissolves conflict and opens the door to forgiveness. When your heart is at peace, free from internal strife, you have more energy to give to the world.

Always give thanks to The Almighty, asking for guidance and to be used as a vehicle for goodness.

3. SWEETNESS OF CONTENTMENT

After my accident, I found myself with only $32 left in my bank account. Yet, instead of despair, I focused on the simple gratitude of being alive. I thanked God for the breath I had and prayed calmly for a solution. Through that contentment, I realised I had been spared for a purpose. I embraced each opportunity, trusting that my path was to serve God and to serve His creation - all of you.

4. POWER OF GIVING

The Prophet Muhammad (peace and blessings be upon him) said, "Give charity without delay, for it stands in the way of calamity." (Al-Tirmidhi, Hadith 589). The act of giving heals not only those who receive but also those who give. By sharing your blessings, you protect yourself and others from life's challenges, creating a ripple effect of positive change.

5. POWER OF UNLIMITED FORGIVENESS

In October 2014, I travelled to India with my family, under the guise of seeking closure for my mother. We had received news from my father's relatives that his days were numbered, and I wanted to give her the chance to say goodbye. Truthfully, my reasons for going were selfish. I didn't care if he lived or not; I just wanted him to survive long enough for my mother to have her moment of closure.

Like many others, my memories of my father were far from good. The word 'dad' felt foreign to me, as though it never had a place in my world. But when I stood by his deathbed, something shifted. As I recited verses from the Holy Qur'an and silently prayed, I found myself pleading, "O my Lord, please do not take him away. I have not done anything for him. Please give me a chance to serve him."

In that heart-wrenching moment, I watched him struggle, his body weak and his eyes rolling upward in pain. He looked terrified, and it broke me. This was a man I barely knew, yet seeing him in such a state was unbearable. All I wanted was for him to have a peaceful end.

To my surprise, something incredible happened within me. A flood of compassion and mercy poured out, a feeling I had never experienced for him before. At first, I thought perhaps it was just my humanity, feeling sympathy as I would for any stranger. But then I realised this was something deeper. I was experiencing love for a man I had known only by name. My heart ached for him, and I couldn't bear the thought of him leaving this world in such a state.

I prayed harder, and to my amazement, a miracle occurred. The next morning, he was revived and moved to the intensive care unit. Hesitant, I went to see him. As I approached, our eyes met. He was still too weak to speak, but there was something in his gaze—joy, perhaps. As I stood by his side, he reached out his frail right hand. Instinctively, I placed mine in his. He pulled my hand to his lips and kissed it.

Those few seconds felt like an eternity. In that brief moment, I felt an overwhelming sense of peace wash over me. It was as if a weight had been lifted from my soul, and all the anger, hurt, and resentment I had carried for so long melted away. My heart was cleansed, and I realised one of life's greatest truths: forgiveness is not just about letting go—it's about freeing yourself from the burden of the past.

Broken things can be blessed things if you let God do the mending.

Our parents are vessels of God, bringing us into this world to fulfil a Divine Purpose. *The moment I released the negative energy I had been carrying for years, it was replaced with love, peace, and compassion for my father. In an instant, he wasn't just my father anymore—he became my daddy, the daddy I never had. It no longer mattered what he hadn't done for me; that moment of connection was everything. Through his near-death experience, God used him to teach me the power of love, mercy, and most of all, the* **Power of Unlimited Forgiveness.**

Though this realisation came more than three decades into my life, I'm deeply grateful to have experienced it. My hope is that children everywhere will learn to cherish their parents, and that parents, too, will understand the lasting impact of their words and actions on their children. Every child is a precious gift, and nurturing their nature with love and care is one of the greatest responsibilities we have.

I am thankful to have reached this place of forgiveness, and I am humbled to have helped many of my coaching clients achieve the same. It isn't easy, but it's not impossible. True healing, I've found, begins with the power of forgiveness. Before we can heal others, we must first heal our own hearts and souls.

Before my trip to India to visit my father, I came across a powerful quote: "Are there broken things you have not taken the time to fix? Are there broken things you have not taken the time to get rid of? If the things in your environment are a reflection of what goes on in your mind, ask yourself, 'Is my mind well-ordered?'"

This struck a chord deep within me. I knew that the one thing I hadn't fixed—the relationship with my father—was holding me back. I realised I couldn't move forward until I freed myself from the emotional prison of anger and resentment. I had to release the pain to find peace.

Thankfully, the moment I set my intention, the universe aligned with me. I was given the chance to seek his forgiveness and offer my own. And miracles truly do happen when we open our hearts. By letting go and trusting in God's plan, I found a new sense of freedom, and life has transformed for me in ways I never imagined.

I believe the same can happen for you. Forgiveness is a powerful force, and once you embrace it, you'll find that life flows with a new kind of peace and purpose. You've got this!

Power of Unconditional Love

Unconditional love is affection without boundaries or expectations—love that exists purely for the sake of love. But how do you know if your love is truly unconditional? Ask yourself, *"Do I love you for who you are, or do I love you for what you give me?"*

Without realising it, relationships can easily become transactional, where we seek to fill a void within ourselves.

This often leads to neediness, clinginess, and unrealistic expectations, which can manifest in hurtful words or even mental strain. If these patterns continue, neither you nor the other person will find lasting happiness.

The key to breaking this cycle is understanding your attachment style and practising healthy boundaries. By doing this, you'll become more grounded, allowing you to love sincerely and selflessly. You'll transform into a vessel for Divine Love, letting it flow through you and into the lives of others.

One of my favourite prayers to help regulate my emotions and keep me grounded is: ***"O Lord, grant me the love of You, grant me the love of those You love, and grant me the actions that lead me to the love of You."***

This simple yet profound prayer reminds me that love is not about what we get, but what we give. When love flows without conditions, it becomes a powerful force for good in the world.

Success Stories

Being Lazy can be a Blessing in Disguise

Personally, I am a very lazy person by nature. Given a choice, I would rather sleep my life away. My family calls me 'The Sleeping Beauty'.

When I meet young people today and I hear a similar remark that they are too lazy to do anything, I will gladly convey to them that being lazy is the first sign of potentially being a successful person.

You may be wondering by now, how does being lazy translate to being a blessing in disguise. Being lazy doesn't mean that you remain stagnant and do nothing at all. You are basically wired differently. You are consciously productive and will creatively find the fastest and most effective way of getting things done with the least amount of time and energy. A task that other people may take weeks to complete, you may accomplish in three days.

And how do you think I emerged as the champion in the 'Surviving the Sky Challenge' organised by the Singapore Cable Car in 2004? In that challenge, I had to live in a cable car for a week. It was not at all comfortable sharing one small cabin with three other people, that too with so many rules and regulations of what we can and cannot do. But I chose to focus on what I do best, that is to just chill and sleep. It felt like a retreat and that led me to winning $50,000 worth of cash and prizes.

Stubborn is Good

In autumn of 2013, I was travelling on board The Reflections 'Celebrity Cruise' for two weeks across Italy, France, Greece, Malta, Turkey, and Spain. Every morning, I woke up to a different port of call with breakfast served in the balcony suite. It's a marvellous experience I wish for every one of you. For the Malta day tour, I learnt about an Ocean Park where you could swim with the dolphins. I was really looking forward to that.

As we were arriving in Malta on a Monday, the cruise crew informed us that unfortunately the park was closed on Mondays and the shore excursion will be cancelled. So nobody from the cruise had a chance to go for that activity. Being the stubborn me who does not take no as an answer, and I was really adamant to swim with the dolphins, my friend and I took a cab and found our way to the park. We knew the park was closed but so what. I insisted that I just wanted to visit the vicinity of the attraction.

We arrived at the entrance and, obviously, the park was closed. I kept knocking on the gate and called out to the staff who passed by the gate. I explained where I came from and that the cruise had to land in Malta on Monday and how I really wanted to swim with the dolphins. To my surprise, she told me to wait a second. I was like, what was she going to do?

Two minutes later, she opened the gate, allowed me in and said, "You can swim with the dolphins and we will open the park for you!" I was awed but kept my cool. It was just my friend and me in the huge park.

The whole experience made me feel like an absolute celebrity. It was about knowing what you want and simply taking action. After the swim with the dolphins, the staff was nice to let us watch a few shows. It was priceless!

"Be stubborn on your goals, and flexible in the journey."

Be the Game Changer: 'Create Opportunities, Value People'

More than anything else, real people in real companies want to be part of a winning team. They want to contribute to producing real results. They want to feel the excitement and the satisfaction of being part of something great. When people begin to feel the magic of momentum and see tangible results, that's when the flywheel starts to build speed—that's when they line-up, throw their shoulders to the wheel, and push. And that is how change really happens.

Power of Teamwork: The Flywheel Effect

In fact, leaders of companies that go from good to great start not with 'where' but with 'who'. They start by getting the right people on the bus, the wrong people off the bus, and the right people in the right seats. And they stick with that discipline—first the people, then the direction—no matter how dire the circumstances. With the right people on the bus, in the right seats, you then turn your full attention to the 'what' question.

VALUES TO LIVE BY

Love Thy Neighbour as you Love Thyself

My dream is to strive for excellence and be able to enable aspiring individuals who want to change the way they live, giving them confidence, responsibility, self-direction, and control over their lives.

I would love for you, as I would love for myself, to build an organisation and have a strong network of people who connect in the spirit of partnership and freedom, not ownership and control. People have a fundamental need to belong to something they can feel proud of. They have a fundamental need for guiding values and a sense of purpose that gives their lives and work meaning.

"Life does not revolve around you alone. Everyone deserves to be equally happy. It is not about having everything to yourself, it is about what you do with what you have."

Be a Celebrity or Leave a Legacy

Empower Humanity: Leading with Purpose and Integrity

In today's world, where fame and recognition often overshadow substance, it's crucial to reflect on the kind of leader we aspire to be. True leadership isn't about flashy titles or celebrity status—it's about resilience, confidence, and compassion. It's about stepping up to serve humanity, not seeking personal glory. A leader driven by substance leaves a lasting legacy, while a leader driven by ego merely chases attention.

The CEOs who transformed their companies from good to great were often anonymous. Is that a coincidence? Not at all. There is a direct relationship between the absence of celebrity and the presence of exceptional results. Why? Because when leadership revolves around one person's ego, the organisation turns into a 'one genius with 1,000 helpers' model, where success seems tied to the individual, not the collective effort.

True greatness in leadership stems from ambition for the work and the greater good, not for oneself. At every critical decision point, the leaders who leave a legacy consistently choose what benefits the organisation, the work, and ultimately, the people. In contrast, celebrity leaders often prioritise their ego, choosing personal recognition over the company's success.

As you continue your journey, ask yourself: Do you want to be a celebrity leader who craves attention or a world-class leader who leaves a lasting, meaningful legacy? The difference lies in whether you aim to serve yourself or humanity. By stepping up, embracing resilience, and empowering those around you, you'll find that true leadership is about service, integrity, and the impact you create in the lives of others.

Giza Pyramids, Egypt
"The Ego is a veil between humans and God. In prayer all are equal."
– Mawlana Rumi

Now is Your Time: Take Action and Commit to Growth

No matter where you are in your journey—whether you're just starting out or expanding an established business—this is your moment to commit fully to your growth. It's time to take personal responsibility, not just for the success of your business or career, but for your own learning, healing, and personal development. Momentum doesn't happen by accident—it's something you build with intention, day by day.

You have the power to create something extraordinary, whether it's a thriving department, a vibrant community, or a meaningful impact in your personal and professional life. Every idea in this book is a tool, but it's up to you to take action and apply them.

Whatever you do, always reconnect with your 'why' – that original spark that fuelled your dream. Take care of your health, nurture your heart, and stay true to the passion that brought you to this point. Let your strengths and purpose guide you. When you're driven by what you love, failure isn't an option – only growth, success, and impact.

The time to act is now. Don't wait for the perfect moment or the ideal conditions; they may never come. Start today. Every small step you take brings you closer to the success and fulfilment you deserve.

BONUS CHAPTER

Conquer

How to Conquer your Fear and Step Up with Confidence?

"Hijab Model & Brand Ambassador for SK Dazzle CSR Campaign – 'Diamonds Are for Everyone!' | Founder & President, Diamond Women Network."

At First I was Afraid, I was Petrified

Since young, I knew deep in my heart that I had the freedom to dream and that I can be whatever I want to be with faith and love. I was creative, multi-talented, loved helping my teachers and friends, and was an active school leader.

Despite my positive persona, I struggled with self-esteem issues due to the name-callings and labels of being the skinny brown kid. Being of mixed origin, I frequently experienced an identity crisis and felt unaccepted. I craved a sense of belonging. I had very few friends and most of the time felt left out. The worst part was putting up an act that everything was alright in my life. I tried to put my feelings aside and tried to be the cool kid.

At home, I bottled all this in silence because I did not want to worry my mother. I was the youngest child of six and somehow subconsciously always felt unloved and unwanted. Perhaps it was the last child syndrome. It did not help my morale that my siblings were better than me academically, and our age gap was so vast.

The Real Problem

Based on Erikson's Stages of Theory, did you know that a child's confidence is being built or broken between the ages of five to twelve years old? This is a real fact and a very serious problem.

Not only are our kids in this age and time terribly affected by external factors like social media and peer pressure, but their inner child - the younger self that may have previously been abused physically, mentally, verbally, and emotionally, is dying and crying within. Just imagine growing up ignoring and numbing all this pain.

This is why many people are unable to embark on what they intend to do, and this is also why most people get started on projects and do not complete them. They somehow always stop halfway.

Does this sound familiar to you? Which of the above categories do you fall into? Do you find it tough to get started on your dream projects, or do you enthusiastically get started yet within weeks, the fire of excitement diminishes rapidly?

Taking Personal Responsibility

Dear precious one, you have to seek knowledge and abide by your roles and responsibilities. It is also the responsibility of your parent, spouse, or child to understand that they have to support you to play the role that you are assigned for. It takes two hands to clap.

You must know that you have the right to live your life on your own terms and not be a puppet. You do not have to prove your abilities to others to gain approval or validation. Take personal responsibility for your healing and growth.

Every Successful Person has a Coach

When I started out, I felt alone, lost, and helpless. It was transformational when I decided to put my foot down and quit the do-it-myself attitude. At the same time, I understood the value of having real mentors to support my dream. And henceforth, I became comfortable with the idea of hiring subject matter experts to assist me in turning my dreams into reality while I intentionally focus on what I do best. I recognised what my genius was. Of course, it was not a simple, straightforward journey, but perseverance does pay off.

Thanks to the many years of trial and error, many hard knocks and falls, I am blessed to have been able to engineer my tried and tested proven system and fit it into my talks, trainings, and my **Signature Mentorship Programme**.

Do you know that you are God's gift and you have a massive role to play in the Universe? To get started, the key is for you to uplift your spirit. How will you do that?

Time is Precious, Use it Wisely

Always remember that it is way easier for us to model an established route and have a guide who has walked the path to hold our hands rather than trying to waste time figuring out how to get started. Here is my '3D System' on how I support my clients to identify where they are and how to get to where they would like to be:

Step 1: Diagnose Yourself

Step 2: Desire Check

Step 3: Decide where you see yourself in 6 to 12 months

"What would you like to do and how would you like to contribute to the world?"

Only you can decide to ignite that light of happiness within you. The only person stopping you is yourself. Stop giving excuses and impede your ability to grow and your capability to maximise your potential. Now is the time!

You Will When you Believe

People with strong beliefs have certain core values that are unchanging. Out of these values emerge deeply held ideals and a defined purpose for their lives. These core values affect their behaviour in many ways. Their sense of mission gives their lives meaning and direction; in their view, success is more than money and prestige.

When you have belief, it gives you direction, guiding you through temptations and distractions towards a consistent set of priorities. Most of the time, the main thing that is holding you back is the **fear of rejection**.

Rejection is God's way of crystallising the clarity of your path to Him. When you are able to accept this, you will transform into a wellspring of powerful drive and direction. You gain confidence, clarity, and stability. That is when you attest to being truly happy.

Stepping Out of the Shell

Do you hate yourself, feel worthless and feel like you are turning into a psycho? How do you intend to regulate this? To keep your sanity, you need to use your creativity and step out of the zone and step up to have at least a half-day in the week to invest in yourself. Be it to pick up a new skill, learn a language, or attend self-development programmes and be around like-minded positive people.

Just because you are instinctively responsible, it might be difficult for you to refuse opportunities. For this reason, you must be selective. Sometimes, you need to remind yourself to say 'no' to others for a big 'yes' to happen for you. Heal yourself first, then set out to heal the world. **Miracles happen to movers.** Get started and be on your way to turning your dreams into reality.

"If you don't love, appreciate and respect yourself, who will?"
Excerpt from '5 Things I Love About Being A Woman'

Glimpse of Excellence

To constantly remind you of your blessings, it is helpful to have photos of your success logs and a glimpse of the excellence of your past achievements. A glimpse of excellence depicts things you have accomplished, which you doubted you could. My biggest pride and joy moment would be to single-handedly bring my wheelchair-dependent mother to the Maldives for a week. I was really fearful at first, doubting myself. The night before the flight, I almost cancelled the trip. Then I just sat and meditated for a few minutes and weighed the options of how much I really wanted to take my mother on a vacation to one of the most beautiful destinations in the world. I remember telling myself, "If I can do this, I can do anything in the world!"

It is said that when you are brave enough to step out of your comfort zone and be willing to take massive action to step up, many doors of opportunities will automatically open for you. Just take the first step. There is no point just staring up the stairs; you've got to Step Up! And truly, upon my return from the Maldives with my mum, that was when I began my journey as a self-published author.

Since then, I have been featured on several media platforms, invited to speaking engagements, and was invited to the Parliament House to meet Madam Halimah Yacob, the President of Singapore.

Zai's first meeting with Madam Halimah Yacob,
President of Singapore

I then engaged mentors and coaches to systemise and grow my training business. It is still a magical snowball effect as I witness the growth of my Step Up Journey. All this can come to light for you just by making a decision to take the leap of faith and consistently doing the do.

Taking the Leap of Faith

Self-belief takes a lot of time to develop, especially to muster the courage to take the first step. With the facilitation of a mentor who resonates with your beliefs and values, it will accelerate an exponential learning curve for you. Remember that your mentor is not present to spoon-feed you. Learn from them, and you have to move forward and take massive action to achieve maximum results.

The Role of a Mentor

Mentors play a similar role to a GPS (Global Positioning System). A GPS is a technical marvel made possible by a group of satellites in Earth orbit that transmit precise signals, allowing GPS receivers to calculate and display accurate location, speed, and time information to the user.

Literally, a mentor is someone who guides you and will unlock your potential and power, and he/she may even draw the map for you based on your passion, strengths, and skills. At this point, you have to decide where your end goal is. Ultimately, you have to be the responsible decision-maker. What would you like to be? Who would you like to serve?

Divorce your Story, and Marry the Truth

Attitude of gratitude is the key to getting started. If we carefully look back at our life journey, there are more moments of happiness and thankfulness to recollect compared to sadness.

When you come to this realisation, you will be able to quit worrying about the future and get past your past stories that are no longer serving you. Learn to silence your mind, live in the present and be in peace. When your heart and mind are filtered and cleared, only then will you be able to focus on getting to your final destination. With confidence and clarity, you will have a smooth sailing journey.

Even if you falter or fail during that journey, you will be able to bounce back and hold your head up high because you know you are super worth it!

What do you Want?

Information or Transformation?

I feel incredibly blessed each time I get the chance to empower even just one person a day. It fills me with pure joy and purpose. Now, let me ask you— are you here only for information, or are you ready for a true life transformation?

If I handed you a magic pen and a blank page, what would be written in your life's script? What would your version 2.0 look like? And if you had the opportunity to start afresh, what would you do differently?

Take a moment to reflect on these five powerful questions to guide your next steps:

1. Where am I at this point in my life?

2. Where do I truly want to be?

3.   What have I tried so far to get there?

4.   Whom can I model myself after, and which mentors can guide me towards my aspirations?

5.   Why did I pick up this book in the first place?

Don't overthink your answers—let your heart speak. Too much analysis can lead to paralysis. Write down whatever comes to mind and flows from within. You don't have to figure this all out alone.

Trying to navigate this journey by yourself can be overwhelming. Without a solid foundation built on your true strengths, there's no point in constructing a glittering structure, no matter how beautiful. Start by identifying your core identity, gaining clarity, and building confidence. When you're at peace with who you are, you will build something lasting and real.

We're not just here to walk this journey alone. We're here to uplift and guide each other—to reflect the greatness within one another. You are not here by accident. You are here by design, created for a purpose that's unique to you.

I invite you now, in this very moment, to **step up** and uncover the resilient, confident, compassionate leader within you. Know this: God did not create you in vain. You have a purpose. Be kind to yourself. Be kind to others. Seek meaning in your purpose and live this precious, fleeting life fully and authentically.

I love you all. Be blessed, stay true to who you are, and take action now.

Step Up Book Tour at Bvlgari Resorts Bali, Indonesia

Congratulations!

By finishing this book, you've taken a powerful step towards transforming your passion into a profitable reality. But this is only the beginning—the journey continues from here. I invite you to explore more with me. Together, we can dive deeper into unlocking your full potential.

Let's Stay Connected!

I'd love to hear from you! Share your thoughts and experiences by writing a review on social media. Use the hashtag **#stepupjourney** and tag **@zai.miztiq** to let me know how this book has impacted you and what action steps you need help with to get started on your journey.

Breaking Chains: A Guide to Reclaiming Your Freedom in Life

Are you ready to reclaim your freedom and take control of your life and business? Scan the code to watch the video and take that next powerful step towards creating the life you deserve.

Looking for More Personalised Guidance?

If you're seeking tailored coaching, mentoring, or hands-on support to fully unlock your potential, I'd be delighted to connect with you. Together, we can transform your passion into purpose and bring your vision to life. To explore more about my work, upcoming events, resources, and coaching services, visit: www.stepupjourney.com.

Scan the QR code below to connect directly and access further resources and updates. Let's continue this journey of growth and success together!

www.ingramcontent.com/pod-product-compliance
Lightning Source LLC
Chambersburg PA
CBHW040804120726

48005CB00012B/1303